Copyright Notice & Disclaimer Notice
(Please Read This Before Using This Book)

CONTENTS

OTHER BOOKS IN THE ESSENTIAL SERIES

Essential Guide to Smart Home Automation Safety & Security

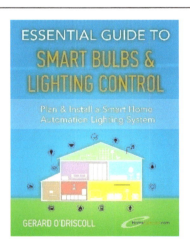

Essential Guide to Smart Bulbs & Lighting Control

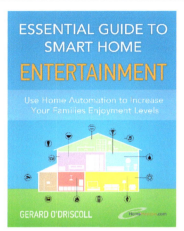

Essential Guide to Smart Home Entertainment

Essential Guide to Smart Homes For Aging Adults

Essential Guide to Nest Smart Home Automation System

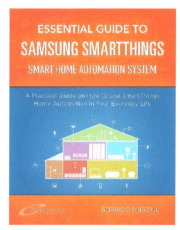

Essential Guide to Samsung SmartThings Smart Home Automation System

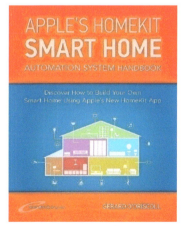

Essential Guide to Apple's HomeKit Smart Home Automation System

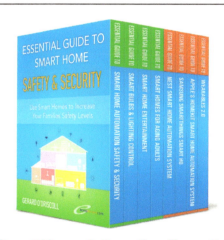

Smart Home Automation Essential Guides Box Set

BEFORE WE BEGIN AND FREE GIFTS

Special Course Offer!

Gerard has recently launched a course titled **Home Automation for Beginners: Create Your Own Smart Home.**

There is currently a limited offer of over 50% off the course with this special link.

Regular price is $147 and you'll get the course for $67!

Click Here to get over 50% discount off the regular price today before the **limited number of coupons run out!**

Home Automation For Beginners: Create Your Own Smart Home **FREE Online Training Workshop**.

International Smart Home Expert - Gerard O'Driscoll has put together a brand new online webinar on how to make your home smarter!

Click Here to Reserve Your Spot Today!

Click Here to Download Your Free Copy of the '8 Week Blueprint on Building a Smart Home'. A summarized action plan, which you can follow over the coming weeks, months and indeed years.

Check Out the Giveaway Here.

WHO SHOULD READ THIS BOOK?

This book is intended to be read by the following people:

- Anybody who wants to learn how to use smart home systems to enhance their families' security & safety levels.

- Professionals and companies who want to grow their business through the installation of smart home security IoT based products.

INTRODUCTION TO USING SMART HOMES TO IMPROVE SECURITY LEVELS

> **❝** *A fully installed Smart Home 2.0 alarm system is a great way of providing us with some peace of mind when away from home.* **❞**

First and foremost, thanks for grabbing a copy of my first book in the 7 book 'Essential Guide to Smart Home Automation' series. Okay, let us get started. Ensuring that your home is safe, especially when crime rates are rising during these recessionary times is extremely important to most of us. Recent data show that a robbery takes place every 15 seconds in the USA!

The repercussions of a break-in can be enormous. In addition to the damage and loss of personal items, people can often experience emotional trauma for months or indeed years after a house burglary.

In my mind burglary protection is one of the most important components of a home automation system. With this functionality, a criminal is less likely to break into your home and steal your prized possessions.

A fully installed Smart Home alarm system is a great way of providing us with some peace of mind when away from home.

As with everything in life, we need to plan our approach to increasing security levels at home; this chapter provides some practical steps.

HOME SECURITY PLANNING

When planning for security around your home, start by thinking like a burglar. Begin outside,, preferably in the evening after the sun has gone down. Look for dark areas around your home. These can be used by potential intruders as hiding areas while they work their way inside. Look for any spot where you might think someone would work on entering your home, including doors, garages, and even second story windows.

All of these locations will need some type of sensor protecting them. When you add a security system, you'll need to plan for covering each of these areas.

Here are six key smart systems that you can use to enhance your family's home security levels:

①   Smart Home Alarm Systems

②   Smart IP Cameras

③   Smart Combo Alarm Devices

④   Smart Access Control Systems

⑤   Smart Locks

⑥   Smart Doorbells

1. Smart Home Automation 2.0 Alarm Systems

Enhancing home security can be as simple as adding the following types of sensors:

- Motion – Used to detect an intruder's presence.
- Glass break – Once a window is broken the sensor sends a signal back to your HA 2.0 controller.
- Door contacts – Once armed, a signal is sent to the controller if the door is unexpectedly opened.
- Window contacts – Operates in a similar manner to door contacts.

These sensors are available as wired or wireless.

An example of a ground floor layout and recommended locations for different types of alarm sensors is presented in Figure 1.

❑ **Figure 1 Smart Home Alarm System – Recommended Sensor Locations**

Once a sensor is tripped by a thief entering your home, a signal is sent to the home automation controller. In addition to setting off the internal siren, the controller will also send you a text message or email, informing you of events as they unfold.

Smart Home alarm systems support some notable features:

- They are operated using an interface such as a touchscreen, keypad, tablet device or a smartphone.

- Highly customisable to meet your security needs – for instance with most Smart Home alarm systems it is up to you to decide the code, the entry delay and exit delay time periods.

- Some systems on the market also allow you to program a phone number of who will be called in case of an alarm. If you are unable to take action, if you do not answer your telephone or if the call is diverted to voice mail, most HA 2.0 products will allow you to specify who is to be called next. When professional monitoring is used, the automation controller contacts the central station, which in turn contacts the appropriate authorities.

- Smart Home controllers provide options for alarm settings when you leave home (AWAY Mode) and when you go to sleep (NIGHT mode).

The types of functionality supported by Smart Home alarm systems include:

● The use of your Smart Home system to monitor, arm and disarm your in-home alarm from anywhere in the world with a smartphone or tablet.

● Disarm your security system automatically when a particular door lock code is entered.

● Arm your security system automatically when other devices are controlled.

● Receive email, text or spoken alerts when any zones are triggered.

Smart Home Alarm Types

In addition to the above, most automation systems also allow you to setup the following alarm types to protect your home:

ABSENCE ALARMS

An absence alarm is used when you leave home for a period of time, for instance heading out to work. As shown in Figure 2 PIN code is generally used to arm an absence alarm.

❑ **Figure 2 Sample Screenshot of Absence Alarm User Interface**

Once you have entered a correct PIN code, the various sensors around the house will be armed. As a result a break-in will initiate the following sequence of events:

 The sensors (door, window or motion) will send signals to your home automation controller.

②   Your controller will activate a loud siren to make things noisy for your intruder and possibly alert a neighbour. Just makes the experience a little less enjoyable for your un-invited guest ☺

③   Depending on how you configured your system, the controller will also send you a notification text message and email.

④   If configured, your absence alarm will also start filming your intruder in action.

NIGHT DETECTION ALARMS

A night alarm allows you to arm specific security sensors when you go to bed. Typical configurations involve the arming of all door, window and glass break detectors. However, motion detectors that pick up movement when you go to the toilet at night are excluded from this type of configuration. This enables you or a family member to get out of bed in the middle of the night and switch on the bathroom light, but also have the alarm armed to protect against someone breaking in.

2. Smart IP Cameras

Before we delve into the topic of connecting an IP camera to your HA 2.0 system, let's take a minute or two to outline the main features of IP cameras:

①   **High quality video content:** IP cameras are digital and produce high-resolution video that is more accurate and clear when compared to viewing an analog video stream.

②   **Indoor and outdoor support:** Indoor IP cameras keep an eye on a particular room whereas outdoor IP cameras are weatherproof and monitor your garden or driveway.

③   **PoE support:** Another cool feature of IP cameras is their support for a networking technology called Power over Ethernet (PoE). This technology integrates power into a standard home networking infrastructure. It enables power to be provided to the network device, such as an IP network camera, using the same cable that is used for the network connection.

④   **PTZ support:** PTZ is an abbreviation for Pan, Tilt and Zoom. As the name implies, this feature allows you to cover quite a large area and get a good overview of what is happening in your home.

⑤   **Wi-Fi support:** Let's not forget about Wi-Fi; IP cameras typically provide Wi-Fi connectivity. In the context of a home automation install, Wi-Fi is the method used to stream images to an automation controller.

⑥ **Two-way audio –** Some IP camera models come with a built-in microphone allowing you to listen to conversations and noises from intruders. In addition to a microphone, some models include an internal speaker or a line out connector that allows you to install some external speakers. Speakers allow you to issue warnings to your intruder in real time whilst he or she is up to no good in your home.

Now that you have zoned in on a particular IP camera make and model, the next step is to physically install and integrate with your home automation controller.

Configuring Your Ip Camera to Connect With Your Controller

For those who have limited computer or IT skills, getting an IP camera up and running can be daunting for some people. Fortunately, the cycle of getting an IP camera to send back streaming video to your iPad or smartphone is relatively straightforward. The key steps required to start using an IP camera are as follows:

STEP 1   **Survey Proposed IP Camera Locations – Power and Network Connectivity**

IP cameras need power and of course they need to wirelessly or over a physical wire connect to a network. The following diagram illustrates three different scenarios.

❏ **Figure 3 Three Different Wiring Scenarios For IP Cameras**

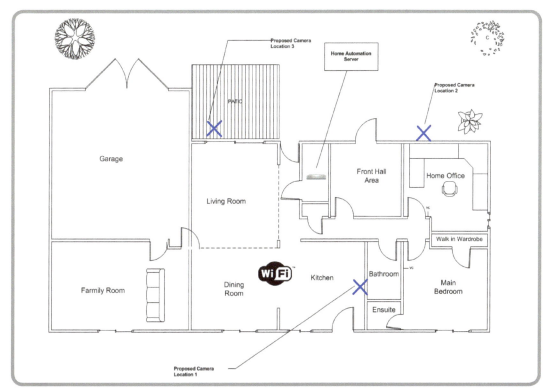

Proposed Camera Location 1: This is easy, basically run a cable to a socket, plug in the camera and it communicates with HA 2.0 controller over Wi-Fi.

Proposed Camera Location 2: The Wi-Fi signal is weak outside, thus a Cat5e cable needs to be run from the broadband router or network switch to this location. From a power perspective, there is a main supply nearby (outside light) and the electrician will be able to install a socket.

Proposed Camera Location 3: No Wi-Fi signal or power cables nearby. Therefore, you will need to run a single Cat5e cable from the broadband router or network switch to this location and use a PoE enabled IP camera.

STEP 2   **Power up and Connect Cables**

As the name implies, you need to ensure that your IP camera is connected to your in-home router and the unit has power.

STEP 3   **IP Camera Discovery**

Once your IP camera is plugged in and the cables are connected in their correct locations, then you use a software program called a 'discovery tool' to allow your PC to access the user interface of the IP camera.

> **Tip:** This software program is typically available on the CD that comes with your IP camera.

STEP 4   **Configure Your PC on the Same Network as your IP Camera**

You now need to ensure that both the PC and IP camera are on the same network. IP addresses (a globally recognised Internet numbering system for identifying electronic devices on a network) form an integral part of this step. It is therefore appropriate that we provide a brief overview of how IP addresses are structured.

An IP address is a series of four numbers separated by dots that identifies the exact physical location of a device such as an IP camera on your network. It is a 32-bit binary number. This binary number is divided into 4 groups of 8 bits ("octets"), each of which is represented by a decimal number in the range 0 to 255. The octets are separated by decimal points. An example of an IP address is 192.168.1.100

Although not evident, the IP address gets split into two separate identifiers:

① the network section is found over on the left-hand side of the number and identifies the network that the IP camera is connected to and

② the host section identifies the actual IP camera

Once the IP camera and your PC are configured on the same network, you can then use a software utility called 'Ping' to verify connectivity between both devices.

STEP 5 Configure Your
IP Camera's Settings

You are now ready to configure the camera's default settings:

• • • • • • ● Type in the camera's IP address, a user-friendly browser-based configuration interface should appear, as shown below:

❑ Figure 4 – IP Camera Home Page Example

Depending on the type of camera, a live feed may also be available on the main home page screen.

The configurable settings will vary between IP cameras; however, here are some common ones:

- Camera parameters, including exposure, white balance, brightness, sharpness, and contrast.

- System settings such as, FTP details, motion detection and network address.

- Streaming parameters including video resolution and compression rates.

STEP 6   Viewing The Camera on Your App

Now that you can access your IP camera from a PC browser, you will no doubt aspire to viewing this video stream on your app. This is a pretty easy task as long as both your IP camera and router support a technology called Universal Plug'n'Play (UPnP). Once you have confirmed that both your IP camera and router are UPnP enabled, you should in theory be able to view your IP camera over the Internet. Before attempting integration of this live feed with your smart home system, it is recommended that you verify that the camera video stream is remotely accessible by typing in the following IP address into your smartphone or PC browser:

http://External IP address of your router: port number (available in your IP camera's documentation).

There is one important observation that you need to be cognizant of when it comes to IP addresses – there are basically two types, namely static and dynamic.

- A *static address* is fixed on your router and does not change.

- A *dynamic address* on your router changes on a regular basis.

Nowadays, most Internet access providers use dynamic IP addressing schemes. To avoid regularly changing the IP address used to remotely access your IP camera, consideration should be given to setting up a service called DDNS. Once configured, DDNS allows you to assign a domain name to your IP camera, which is always discoverable even if your router uses dynamic IP addresses.

Now that you have proven that your camera is contactable over the Internet, you need to update your HA controller to include details of your new IP camera.

3. Smart Combo Alarm Devices

Traditional surveillance and security concepts have undergone an explosion of new ideas brought on by the arrival of smart technology. It's more than an improvement of camera sensors to include night vision capabilities and high-definition clarity.

This is the coupling of internet connectivity, home automation, and advanced security features all in one compact package. These combined packages are evolving into a new home security category of devices called 'smart combo alarms'.

About Smart Combo Alarm Devices

They are packed with the kind of sensory technology that you might expect in a small robot. The hardware components fit in your hand. Some key elements of a smart combo alarm device include:

An IP Camera - A camera acts as an all-seeing eye, capturing superbly detailed video that's compressed and stored. Connected by WiFi to the internet, the video is stored in the cloud or watched live on your smartphone. Here are the main features of an effective smart camera.

- Motion detector equipped to activate the camera when an event occurs.

- Furnished with a sensitive microphone.

- WiFi internet connectivity.

- Flexible App program sets rules for security.

- Optional extras including temperature monitoring and a siren.

- GPS enhanced. Turns off the system when the smartphone approaches.

- Learns to ignore pets and identify common household events.

A Motion Detector - They're cameras that support the latest in optical technology, often outfitted with a motion detector to ensure the camera is only triggered when there's suspicious movement in your home.

A Home Automation Interface – Smart combo alarm products can also act as your home automation controller, allowing you to setup various types of security scenes to enhance protection around your home. Automation choices are close to unlimited, leaving you completely in control of home security whether you're at the office or at the beach enjoying your vacation. Go even further thanks to considerable effort and forethought on the manufacturer's part, and create lists of trusted users that can access your home if they have the App installed.

How to Install?

These sentinels of home surveillance require little to no installation. Bring out a few tools to fix the combo camera and alarm unit to the wall and you're done. Here are some key installation steps:

① Fix each one to a surface and angle the camera to cover the area of concern, make finite adjustments until you're satisfied.

② There's likely to be a power cable to plug in. Do this and check to see if the unit has a backup battery. Ensure these batteries have been fitted, and start configuring your security.

③ You'll have to download the App and setup the WiFi connection to your router.

④ Check to make sure that the WiFi signal is okay.

⑤ Finish by setting access and alarm rules in your new smartphone App.

Your home safety is paramount, and this is reflected in the design of these smart devices. With flexibility and high-tech convenience, many cameras can be installed to cover every vulnerable spot that occupies your security-aware concerns. Mount them and connect everyone to your home network within minutes. Create alarm rules to send you an alert if there's movement. Set another rule to turn on the camera and alert you when a door is opened. Respond by touching an App button and monitor the situation, live by choosing the next action yourself.

Smart Combo Alarms Practical Usage Example

When your newly installed smart combo security alarm hears a noise on its microphone or detects movement through the optical lens, the camera is triggered, recording video from the area where this mystery activity takes place. The high-definition footage acts on the rules you set, sending an alert demanding your attention, activating a live feed. Ultimately in control, you monitor the situation, avoiding false alarms. Maybe a friend has dropped by unexpectedly, and you tap a control to drop the alarm back into active standby. Alternatively, the rule could be far more exacting, setting off the siren and alarm as soon as a window or door is compromised.

4. Smart Access Control Systems

Secure and effective access to your home is absolutely essential in today's world; particularly in these recession times! In addition to automating your lights, alarm, entertainment, heating and blinds, why not set your home apart by installing some type of access control system that you could used to determine the following:

- Who is allowed to enter or exit your home?

- Which doors they can use to enter or exit your home?

- What time of the day or night family members are allowed entry and exit?

How a Smart Access Control System Works

The addition of access control to your Smart system can heighten security levels and provide an extra layer of convenience.

The major components of a typical Smart access control system are illustrated in Figure 4.5 and explained in the following paragraphs.

❏ **Figure 5 Smart Access Control Architecture**

Access control cards – Stores the 'who where and when' access control information. Popular form factors include plastic fob and cards.

A card reader at each door – This piece of hardware reads the configuration data from control cards and sends back to the home automation controller. When presented with a valid card, the reader can initiate the following actions:

● Open the door ☺

● Arm or disarm your alarm system.

● Activate various home automation scenes

A remotely controllable electronic lock – As the name implies this unit secures your door. It requires power, typically 12 or 24 volts.

A cable that runs from the card reader back to your automation controller – As illustrated a cable (I normally use Cat5) is run between the automation controller and the access reader. Two of the wires are used to carry power and two more are used for the purpose of carrying control data. The other 4 wires are spare.

Once the above items are installed correctly and configured, a smart home door and access control system allows you to do the following:

• • • • • • ● Check the status of your door locks from your smartphone; great peace of mind feature!

• • • • • • ● Monitor and control your door locks from anywhere with an Internet-enabled device.

• • • • • • ● Remotely allow access to your home or holiday home for local tradesmen.

• • • • • • ● Locks your doors automatically based on factors such as the time of day and occupancy status.

• • • • • • ● Receive notifications on your phone when the kids arrive home from school.

• • • • • • ● In the event of an emergency (a fire for instance), your access control system can automatically open all doors.

In addition to all the serious elements of access control listed, there are also a couple of fun and enjoyable elements to installing access control readers on your front and back doors:

 No more need to fumble around for your keys – swiping a card is easy!

 Secondly, you can configure these systems to trigger different scenes. Once installed, why not configure your system to turn on your favorite Internet radio station, when you swipe your card coming home from work.

5. Smart Locks

> ❝*The relationship between smart locks extends beyond the home thanks to a Wi-Fi enabled internet connection*❞

Fumbling for your front door key after a long day is a familiar ritual.

It's dark, you're hungry, and you finally grabbed the right key, but now you can't locate the keyhole.

What a frustrating situation. Now imagine a system that instantly recognizes you as you approach, turns on the entry light above the front door, and opens the door with a reassuring snap of smooth mechanical motion.

It's time to embrace this concept, and drag the age-old lock into the 21st century.

The Benefits of Smart Locks

It focuses purely on those approved to enter your home, on people rather than a dumb piece of metal, smart locks use advanced recognition technology, access codes, combinations of Wi-Fi and Bluetooth, all to simplify and hasten your entry to the sanctuary of your home.

Smart locks are always on guard, waiting for an encrypted virtual key to be transmitted from your smartphone, or for the tapped access code to be entered into a tiny keypad.

By contrast, compare a traditional lock and key with smart locks.

Several vulnerabilities come to mind. A key can be lost or misplaced. A key can be copied in minutes at a hardware store. Smart locks, on the other hand, use security protocols designed for bank systems, digital encryption technologies that can't be copied or broken.

Let's take an introductory look at what intelligent design brings to locks.

After the primary feature of security comes convenience, customization, and remote access.

Next generation smart locks blend these features, using advanced wireless connectivity to form an identifying link between themselves and any smartphone equipped with the security App and virtual key.

Convenience crosses over to customization by including software and hardware options to hook up the lock to household smart systems, communicating with any other smart object in order turn on household lighting and heating, all dependent on personalized settings.

The relationship between smart locks extends beyond the home thanks to a Wi-Fi enabled internet connection that allows you to run everything while at work or stuck in traffic.

And finally smart locks can operate as a standalone without the need to purchase a whole house automation system.

Options for Smart Locks

Each smart lock is a balance of technological features and familiar operation. There are three different approaches that you might want to consider, when researching smart locks, namely:

①   You can keep your traditional key, and opt to add a smart lock as an extra layer of security.

②   Replace the entire assembly with a hybrid of technology and tradition in the shape of an illuminated keypad. Your only responsibility now is to remember to give every member of the family an access code. Don't forget or you'll have angry family members to deal with!

③   The final alternative is the second generation smart lock, a highly connected intelligent lock, one that drops keys and codes in favor of sensors and recognition software. This generation of lock detects the nearness of an occupant or guest carrying a wireless digital key stored in your smartphone.

How Smart Lock Systems Work?

A simplified diagram depicting the main elements of a smart locking system are presented in Figure 4.6 and described in the following sections.

Figure 6 - Component of a Smart Locking System

Smart
Lock

①

Wireless Signal (Wi-
Fi, NFC or BLE

Broadband
Router

Smart Home
Automation
Controller

Electronic FOB

Smart
Lock App

③

②

① THE SMART LOCK ITSELF

Although smart locks come in a variety of styles, technologies, and finishes, they still use secure mechanical components made from toughened steel and tamper-proof alloys.

Smart locks also include an electronic component, making it the potential weak link in the system.

However, rest assured, manufacturers use several layers of digital security to make all smart locks completely secure. Encrypted smartphone signals use 256-bit codes to unlock the door, the latest Bluetooth and Wi-Fi protocols should provide you with some peace of mind against electronic penetration by an intruder.

The physical components sit behind the smart lock, safe within your home. The enclosure is a compact, complex arrangement of interfacing electronics, computer hardware, and moving parts, including a motorized drive. A power assembly, energized by a set of batteries or live current, brings your smart lock to life. When the access signal is approved, the motor activates the pins and tumblers (slotted rotating discs), and draws back the bolt.

The mechanical components share an affinity with traditional lock parts, but the electronic hardware is what defines the lock's smartness. The circuitry triggers an unlock deadbolt event when it senses the nearness of the correct electronic code, whether entered directly on a keypad or sent over the air from a smartphone.

② SMARTPHONE & APP

Similar to other smart home systems an App is typically used to interact with your smartphone. The app is used for initial setup. Other uses include:

- Wirelessly sending an electronic key to the lock.

- Disabling and deleting electronic keys.

- Accessing history of smart lock activity.

Wi-Fi or Bluetooth is normally used to establish a dependable wireless link between your smartphone and the smart lock installed in the door

③ A SMART FOB

Some people prefer to use a FOB to open and close their smart locks. Some key features of smart lock FOBs:

- Unlike traditional fobs, these smart lock fobs are able to hold electronic keys.

- The form factor is relatively small and is comparative to their mechanical counterparts.

- Although rare nowadays smart FOBs can be provided to someone who needs to access your home but does not use an up to date smartphone – your parents, daughter or son for instance.

- Smart FOBs are fully mangeable. In other words, you give a smart FOB to a contractor doing work in your house and set it up to only allow access at certain times of the day and week - Monday - Friday, 8am - 5pm for instance.

- It is more challenging for potential intruders to make copies of smart FOBs. In the olden days, all an aspiring 'burgularpreneur needs to do was copy your front door key at the hardware store.

In the event of a Smart FOB getting lost, it's pretty straightforward to go into the Smart Lock software (typically running on the Cloud) to deactivate the FOB. No more need to go through the expensive process of changing door locks.

Smart locks possess built-in management software to distribute power to low-current components, normally replaceable alkaline batteries available at any store. When those batteries do eventually run low, the lock can be set to send an alert to your smartphone or flash a message on the display of the lock.

Installing a Smart Lock

The term Do-It-Yourself is perhaps thrown around too much. Fortunately, smart locks are simple to install, it requires no alterations to your doors. They're designed to be retrofitted, to be fixed in the same location, using the same openings as your previous lock. Just follow the four steps described below:

① Mount the lock just as you would a traditional lock, and take care to ease the front display panel and delicate electronics into place.

② Now, take a few minutes to fit the batteries and configure the software.

③ Follow the instructions step-by-step to set all functions and features, a little like setting up a computer peripheral.

④ Download the App and test the lock.

Day-To Day Smart Lock Application Scenarios

With smartphone Apps and intelligent software and hardware running the home, there are countless ways to customize your smart locks – here are some that worth considering once your smart lock is up and running:

① Assign codes to guests that expire after 24 hours.

② Access the Web application and set the environmental controls to activate when a family member arrives home.

③ Configure the smart lock to sense presence and automatically unlock when you are in within a few feet of your front door.

④ Send text and email alerts to your smartphone or tablet to display certain events, such as a power outage or a possible intruder alert.

⑤ Use your own smartphone to send access codes to the cell phones of contractors or housekeepers.

⑥ Set video cameras to take stills of guests as they arrive to a party, and instantly unlock the door for them.

⑦ During school time, setup the smart lock to send out a notification when your kids arrive home in the evening.

6. Smart Doorbells

There's no part of the modern home that isn't touched in some way by smart technology. This isn't a quirk of futuristic science destined for a dead end. Smart products are a rapidly maturing line of appliances and devices being manufactured by world-leading companies, and the doorbell is next to be made over, recreated with wireless connectivity and additional functionality.

The Coming of the Smart Doorbell

Push the button on your boring, conventional doorbell and you blindly walk your hallway with a frown of puzzlement. The chime has caught your attention, but you have no idea who's at the door. This accepted routine is being entirely rewritten by the latest generation of smart doorbells. Firstly, when the illuminated doorbell is depressed, you're no longer blind to who's out there. A smart doorbell has digital sight, the ability to transmit video of the person outside through a WiFi connection thanks to a built-in camera. This alone is a blessing in our security conscious age, but you also have the option to talk to the person through an integrated intercom.

While basic approaches to practical smart doorbells act as little more than a high-tech intercom, fully-equipped models are high-security concepts granting convenience and safety with WiFi connectivity. You can check who's at the door from the comfort of your, by picking up your smartphone to see video of the potential guest and be able to make a decision to allow entry by switching to your smart lock App. If you don't recognize the face, tap another button and converse with the stranger to learn why they're intruding on your precious quiet time.

It may seem like a lazy way to answer the door, but think of the advantages. Instead of lazing on your couch, you might instead be on vacation or stuck at work. The point is, your voice issues from the little speaker on the smart doorbell, leaving the person at the door with the impression of you inside your home. This is security through awareness with a healthy dose of wireless magic.

PRACTICAL USAGE EXAMPLES

A smart home system can be customized to meet your daily living needs. The following examples describe how some of our customers are using HA 2.0 products to solve particular problems and enhance their living.

Implementation Example 1 – Enhancing Security Levels of an Elderly Couple in the UK

Requirement

An elderly couple in Birmingham, UK connected with us earlier this year and outlined that they wanted to upgrade their existing HA 2.0 system to automatically switch three lights on in the house when motion is detected in their back garden. Here is the solution that was used:

The Solution

① Their local electrician installed standard outside lights that includes motion detection functionality, which triggers locally once an intruder starts to move closer to the main house.

② These mains powered sensor lights are pretty standard and in reality do very little to deter a thief from entering the premises, so I suggested that they add an outdoor Z-wave motion sensor in the desired location. In this case as illustrated in Figure 3.7 the sensor is mounted to an outside wall on the extension.

❑ Figure 7 Implementation Example 1

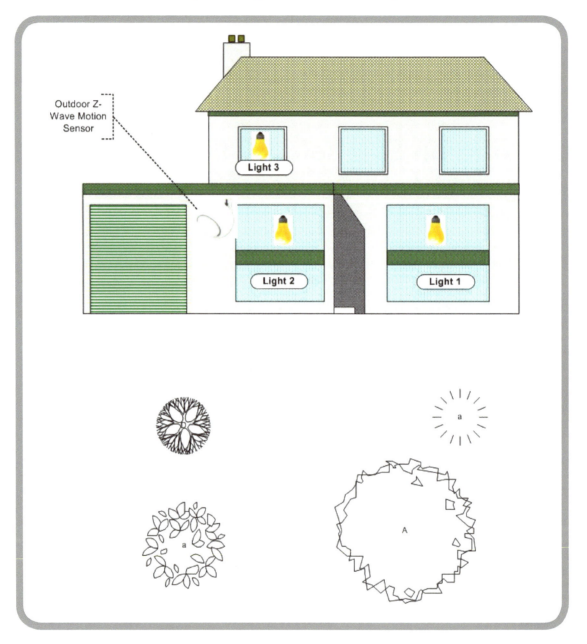

Outdoor Z-Wave Motion Sensor

Light 3

Light 2

Light 1

③ The electrician included the new sensor in the elderly couples existing in-home Z-Wave Smart Home network.

④ A scene was setup to turn on three internal lighting circuits for a period of 10 minutes once the outdoor motion sensor detects an intruder on the couple's property.

Please note that this scene can also be expanded in the future by editing the configuration to set off more lights, turn on a siren, play music or even activate a camera!

The elderly couple now have added another measure that will hopefully act as a deterrent for anybody considering a break-in to their property.

Implementation Example 2 – Create the 'Lived In' Look

Requirement

We had another homeowner (Owen based in West Cork) who has used standard light timers over the years to make his house look like it was lived in, whilst away on holidays. With the recession and increase in crime rates, Owen asked for some advice on how to transfer this functionality over to an automation system. Here is the solution that was used:

Solution

A simplified graphical view of the solution used by Owen is illustrated Figure 8 and explained in the following steps:

❑ **Figure 8 Implementation Example 2**

①   Owen got his electrical contractor to install some wireless light dimmers, switches and plug-ins around the house.

②   He purchased a Smart Home controller online and configured a scene called 'Lived In' to turn lights on and off in particular rooms at random times during the evening – gives the illusion that there is a family member at home.

③   When Owen and his family are away for any extended period of time he activates the 'Lived In' scene when leaving the house, making the house look as if it was occupied.

It is hard to say for definite whether the above solution deters would-be thieves from monitoring his house. However, from sa personal interaction with him the above solution has certainly enhanced his peace of mind when he is out of the house.

INTRODUCTION TO USING SMART HOMES TO IMPROVE SAFETY LEVELS

Smart Homes are synonymous with entertainment and increasing your security levels, but can they make life safer at home?

In fact they can not only reduce risks to you or your family's health but can also prevent costly damage to your house caused by extreme temperatures and leaking water.

The sections below give an overview of 3 key systems that you should consider implementing to enhance your property's , safety and the health levels in your house.

INSTALL SMART SMOKE DETECTORS

Did you know that nearly a billion smoke and carbon monoxide detectors are installed in homes and businesses across the United States?

The purpose of this army of smoke detectors is to make an effort to be proactive in staving off disaster and emergency calls.

Half of the country is required by the law to make carbon monoxide detectors a standard feature, a trend that will continue to spread.

Well over half of the fire-related deaths that occur in the nation can be blamed on faulty smoke detectors, indicating that there is a need for innovations from creative minds.

Smart homes add an extra layer of safety for families through their support for smoke alarm systems that are used to detect fire and alert the occupants of the house immediately. A smart smoke alarm lies at the heart of your smart home safety system and makes a loud noise once fire is detected.

Additionally, it sends a signal to your home automation controller, which in turn will also make a loud noise and send an SMS, email or telephone notification to you about this alarm.

Smart Smoke Detector Features That Could Save Your Life!

Here's a close-up look at ten cool smart smoke alarm features that could save your life and avoid future 911, 112 or 999 emergency calls.

 ### Smart Smoke Alarms Send out Advanced Alerts Once Your Battery Starts to Degrade

One of the biggest problems responsible for thousands and indeed millions of emergency calls around the world is smoke alarm battery failure. If we delve in deeper, research has shown that battery failure is often due to people forgetting to change their batteries. This means that in most homes the smoke alarm batteries may not be in great shape. Thanks to smart smoke detectors, these units will actually make you aware that there is cause for concern and that you need to install fresh batteries before disaster strikes.

 ### Smart Smoke Alarms Interface with your Smartphone

Most people nowadays are tied into mobile devices. Thus, when the alarm is sounding or the batteries are low, a message will be sent to your mobile device. Rather than waking you in the middle of the night with that aggravating low-battery chirp, you'll be alerted in a timely manner and be able to take care of the problem.

Useful functionality when away from home because you'll be alerted to problems and can immediately request the emergency services.

 ### Smart Smoke Detectors Send Out an Early Warning Signal

Before danger strikes and smoke or carbon monoxide levels are creeping up, a smart smoke alarm system can be configured to send out a first warning sign. You can then respond, investigate if there truly is a problem, and take care of matters before a full-blown emergency takes place.

 ### Smart Smoke Alarms Can Be Deactivated With A Wave

The next time a burning toast sends up a cloud of smoke and sets off the alarm, some smart smoke detectors supports the 'hand waving' function. A simple wave of the hand will turn OFF the alarm when there is no true emergency.

Enjoy A Night Light as an Added Perk

Some of the more advanced smoke detectors come equipped with LED lights that will actually provide enough illumination to be a night light. It's perfect for young children who need extra security if they should awaken in the dark.

A Vocal Warning is An Effective Combination with an Alarm

Time and again, an emergency call has come in for another fire-related disaster involving children who did not awaken when the smoke alarm sounded. No one wants to answer 911 calls to discover there has been a terrible injury or a dreadful death. According to research, youngsters respond best to a voice, particularly a female voice that reminds them of their mother. As a result, some of the smart smoke detectors have a female voice that alerts members of the household that there is a problem, in addition to a loud alarm.

Smart Smoke Alarms Have A Wireless Interconnect Feature

Most family homes will have more than one smoke detector, while businesses have an impressive network. A typical smart smoke alarm includes a wireless interconnect feature, ensuring that every alarm will communicate with each other. If there is a problem in one room in the household, all the rest of the alarms will sound as well.

The main point is to send out an alert to every possible area in order to make sure an emergency call will be made after everyone has made it to safety.

Supports a Combination of Sensors

High-end smart smoke detectors include an array of sensors that provide you with a level of protection beyond compare.

Enjoy the Flexibility of More Than One Language

Recognizing the fact that the world contains a cultural blend, the advanced smart smoke alarms will communicate in the language of your choice. It's a simple matter of programming the preferred language upon installation.

Integrate into Smart Home Scenes

It is also possible to set off various scenes once the smoke sensor is activated. For instance, you are able to configure your HA 2.0 controller to turn on certain lights in the house at a particular dim level to help your family find their way through the darkness and escape to the outside.

Smart Smoke Detectors Install Tips

Here are some tips with regards to installing wireless Smart smoke alarms:

- If fire is a personal concern, then you need to consider installing a smoke alarm in each of the rooms.

- If you live in a two storey house there should be at least one smoke alarm for each floor.

- As illustrated in Figure 9, you need to locate smoke alarms in close proximity to bedrooms.

❑ **Figure 9 Typical Locations for Smart Smoke Alarm Units**

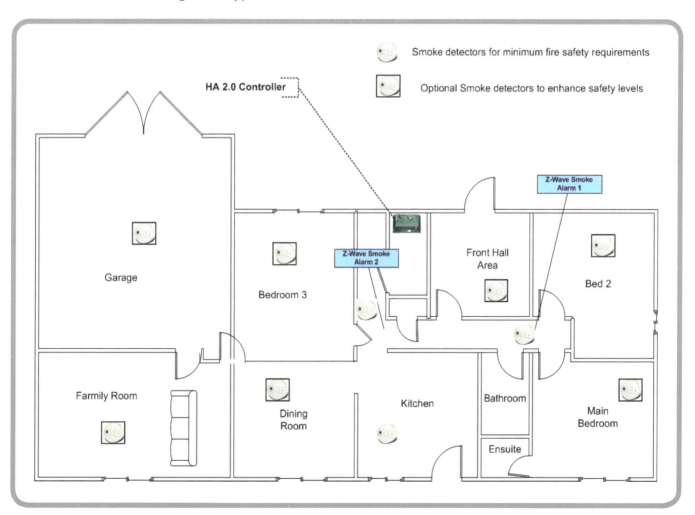

ADD WATER & FREEZE DETECTION

The establishment of a water alarm system involves the installation of a flood sensor. Once water flooding is detected an alert is sent straight back to your home automation controller. Water can originate from a number of sources ranging from leaking pipes to refrigerators.

Similar to the smoke alarm system, once the water sensor detects problems, your home controller will emit a loud sound and notifications are sent onwards via email, SMS and telephone calls.

Here are the steps associated with installing a flood detection sensor and interfacing with your Smart Home controller.

① For a start, your Z-Wave alarm flood detector needs to be physically installed. These units typically comprise of two parts – a sensor located on the floor and a transceiver, which is placed high up on the wall to maximize signal strength. Note that both parts are interconnected via a cable.

② The next step is to put your controller into Include mode.

③ Undo and remove the screw from the bottom edge of the transceiver. Remove the back cover and fit appropriate batteries.

④ The next step is to press the link key three times within a short period (i.e. 1 to 2 seconds).

⑤ The icon for the flood detector will appear on your controller's interface.

⑥ Next step is to enter a desired name for the flood detector.

⑦ Click Save to save all settings for this device.

Freeze alarm sensors are also available that will work with your existing Smart Home system and send out alerts if freezing conditions are detected. This will improve your peace of mind and help to protect against burst pipes during periods of extreme cold. Please note that combined water and freeze detectors are available for purchase.

Implementation Example – Receive a Text message and E-mail When a Water Leak is Detected

REQUIREMENT

An example of how people are using Smart Home systems to solve specific problems involves a rack of expensive AV equipment located in a utility room! Basically, a family in Northern France, installed a sophisticated Home Automation system in their home. . Everything works perfectly fine, however the centralized rack that houses their music server, structured wiring modules, home cinema receiver and multi-room amplifier is in close proximity to their washing machine. In their email to me, they outlined concerns with regards to the risk of the washing machine leaking and causing thousands of Euro worth of damage to the equipment stored in the rack.

Here is the solution that was used:

THE SOLUTION

A simplified block diagram depicting how this problem was resolved is illustrated in Figure 10 and explained in the steps below:

❑ **Figure 10 Implementation Example Water Flooding**

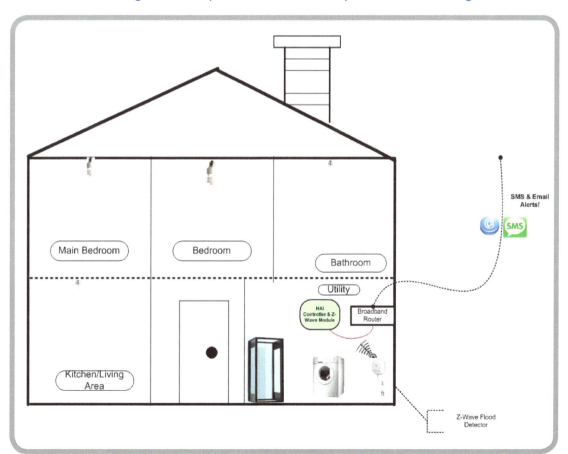

The homeowner purchased and mounted a wireless water sensor to the wall in the utility room.

① The homeowners had installed a wired based home automation during construction.

② In order to interconnect the wireless sensor to the main controller a gateway module was used to pass alerts to the controller.

③ The Smart Home automation controller was programmed to send email and SMS messages once the water detector is triggered.

④ An App now informs them immediately if their washing machine springs a leak.

INSTALL A SMART HOME AIR HEALTH MONITORING DEVICE

> **❝***Our ideal home is a sanctuary from the outside, keeping the dangerous aspects of the natural world from entering.***❞**

Have you any idea or even thought about the quality of air that you breathe at home? To be honest, it never crossed my mind until I was made aware in recent weeks that 'bad air' is a major cause of cancer and a danger to people's general well being. Bad air is best defined as air that consists of a mixture of harmful emissions, particles, pollen and natural airborne enemies that threaten you or your family's health.

Our ideal home is a sanctuary from the outside, keeping the dangerous aspects of the natural world from entering. On the whole, we succeeded in our mission, creating a bright and clean atmosphere that's fresh and safe for the whole family. But evolution finds ways to penetrate your household boundaries, entering the structure of the most modern home, mostly in the air you breathe. Invisible spores float through clean rooms as mold incubates in wet, isolated spaces.

The Dangers of Indoor Air at Home

Unfortunately, there are plenty of household systems and materials that are potential threats to air quality. Rising smoke from a burning fire is a far greater hazard than the soon to follow heat. Carbon monoxide fumes are invisible and insidious, often not acted upon until it's too late. You need peace of mind from these hazards, from toxic fumes and the build-up of gas caused by damaged or blocked heating vents. A smart guardian is the solution, a cutting-edge device that's on watch 24-hours a day.

No one wants health-compromising fungi and spores triggering asthma attacks, or life-threatening smoke and toxic fumes endangering family members. Let's take a look at options for guarding against these dangers by investigating two smart air quality management devices:

1. Smart Indoor Air Quality Monitors

Your first line of defense is a sensor capable of sniffing out airborne pollutants, the risk factors the naked eye can't see. Potentially toxic contaminants are detected by a compact sensor that otherwise fades aesthetically into the background of the room it occupies. Packed with the latest, most sensitive sensory circuitry, this class of device is designed to monitor specific factors of the air you breathe. Levels of particulate matter, moisture density, are all precisely measured and transmitted to a mobile App for your scrutiny.

Benefits and Features of Smart Air Quality Monitoring Devices

Table 1 summarizes the principal advantages of a smart air quality monitoring device.

❏ Table 1 Key Benefits of Smart Air Quality Devices

Constant monitoring of air quality.
Wellness focused detection of contaminants.
Superior detector of smoke, carbon monoxide and carbon dioxide
WiFi and Bluetooth connectivity.
Manageable using Smartphone and tablet Apps.

Push alerts and text warnings.

Comprehensive data tracking displays about your home air content on the App.

Built-in audio and visual alarms if air quality is dangerous.

Preventing health problems, guarding against fire; smart air monitoring is the logical future of air monitoring in the home. These devices guard warn of allergens and contaminants - transmitting the results by Wi-Fi or Bluetooth to a detailed display on your mobile device. Easily see the moisture levels and peaks of invasive particles in your home air.

How They Work and Setup?

For the health and safety conscious, these devices pack multiple sensors into a small design. Core electro-chemical technology interfaces with embedded software to measure levels of specific pollutants, passing the relevant data to a Wi-Fi chip, which in turn relays the data as a filtered and organized set of information displayed on your monitoring App.

Configuration is simply the fixing of the device in the living space, although some designs are surface mountable, and follows a step-by-step setup to hook the device to the Wi-Fi network and your App. Batteries are required, and we all know the annoyance of forgetting to replace them, but smart home technology within the monitor is programmable with the touch of a button to send an alert when battery life is running low.

2. Smart Mold Detectors

Whatever the reason, be it locality, a leaking water pipe, or an undetected environmental factor, mold and mildew will happily settle into your home. The cost of this growth is property damage and impurities in the air. Every member of the family will likely suffer from varying degrees of respiratory distress as the spores ejected from the mold enter heating ducts and find their way into living spaces. This reduction in air quality is especially hazardous to those in the household with breathing conditions, such as asthma and allergies. A smart mold detector intelligently measures these threats through moisture analysis, allowing you to take action before health problems develop.

Dangers of Moisture in the Air

By the time spores reach your lungs, causing throat irritation and allergic reactions, the mold has already developed a strong potency, even though all may look well.

Mold may be a stubborn irritant, but it can't survive without the presence of moisture. The fungi prospers rapidly in a wet environment, spreading and releasing harmful spores into the air. The reason for the moisture could be the humid atmosphere of a wet climate or damaged plumbing, air-conditioning, creating an imbalance in household moisture levels.

How Smart Moisture Detection Work

The solution to mold is a detector that seeks out moisture behind baseboards and wall cavities, in the cracks of drywall and the hidden passages where pipes travel. When damp strikes, the device recognizes a change in room moisture, employing an active chemical compound capable of high orders of sensitivity. Hidden wet spots are instantly recognized, indicating an approximate location, perhaps just below the surface of a wall, where wetness is feeding growing fungi. The sensor design triggers an alarm as a warning of potential mold growth. Install it in a suspect location, a bathroom or utility area, and feel satisfied that you're family is protected from dangerous molds. Some key features of smart mold detectors are shown in Table 2:

Table 2 – Smart Mold Detector Characteristics

Detects moisture before molds can gain traction.
Active chemical sensor.
Triggers an alarm when hidden wetness is found.
Smart technology checks to see if moisture is present for 48-hours or longer before activating alarm.
Battery powered and easy to install

THINGS TO REMEMBER

In this book, here are the key take away points to remember:

- Smart Home systems can be pre-programmed to allow you to remotely monitor, arm and disarm your alarm using a smartphone, PC or tablet device.

- If the Smart Home alarm is set off, you will be automatically informed by e-mail, text or indeed phone of a break-in.

- Wireless combo alarm devices hooked up to the internet represent cutting-edge peace of mind at your fingertips.

- IP cameras allow you to view live video images on your smartphone. Additionally, they can be configured to record live video when an alarm is detected.

- Access Control offers a secure, convenient, flexible and cost effective way of controlling who has access to your home and when that access is allowed.

- Replace existing locks, quickly substituting them with smart locks without making any changes to your door, turning home access into an exhilarating experience as your lock welcomes you, identifying you by name. The door unlocks and lights are turned on to give you a warm welcome. No more key fumbling, only safe, secure and smart entry.

- Wireless and Internet connected, smart doorbells can be answered from anywhere. The addition of the camera is a perfect coupling of technology that works well with a smartphone, delivering total awareness of who's at your door. Combine the technology with the new generation of wireless locking mechanisms, and you have ultimate control.

- The installation of smoke alarms increases your families' safety levels by providing you with an early warning of fire.

- Smart smoke alarms are breaking new ground, paving the way to fewer emergency calls thanks to improvements that will make others take notice and could revolutionize the industry. They are an excellent addition to your home, well worth the investment.

- Once integrated onto your Smart Home network, water and freeze sensors can send you warning alerts.

- Once installed an air quality monitor can wirelessly warn you of any number of pollutants, while innovative smart mold detectors guard against accumulations of mold-feeding moisture. This is crucial for family members who may be suffering from respiratory problems such as asthma or even elderly people who are impacted negatively by bad air circulating in their homes.

ABOUT THE
AUTHOR

Gerard O'Driscoll is 45 years old and originally from Cork in Ireland, married to Olive with five kids ranging from 3 to 14 years old — so a busy house!

Over the past 20 years, Gerard has served in a variety of management, engineering, and commercial positions in both public and private sectors. Gerard is an accomplished international telecoms expert, educator, and serial Internet entrepreneur as well an angel investor. Other professional achievements include the authoring of various books:

Over the years, Gerard has been given the role as a commentator on industry events, and trends in the various industry sectors and has been quoted in a number of premier business publications. Additionally he has presented papers at a handful of conferences around the world.

In recent years, Gerard has become involved as an angel investor in a portfolio of start-ups & emerging growth companies in mobile apps, e-commerce, e-Learning, subscription commerce, food, Wearable and digital home sectors.

DEDICATION

Apparently, behind every important guy is a great girl.☺ This book is dedicated to that girl — my loving wife and girlfriend for over 20++years — Olive!

Of course my dedication extends to our five precious children:

- » Aoife (our little GAA star)☺
- » Ciara (Our little fashion queen)
- » Gerard (AKA Gerdie the hard man)
- » Dearbhla (Our 4 year old little princess)
- » And Baby Aoibhinn (our little Thumbelina, who is now in the terrible two's!).

Also a big dedication goes to my Mother and Father living in Dear Old Skibbereen, West Cork; and my two younger brothers — Owen and Brian. And finally my Electronic Production drinking buds!

WOULD YOU LIKE TO HEAR MORE ABOUT SMART HOMES

We're on the cusp of smart home automation becoming really popular. Nearly everything in your house can be connected. Your garage door, your washer and dryer, your lights, thermostat, door locks, sprinkler system, shades, and more. HomeMentors provide various options in terms of books, courses, and events to increase your knowledge of this space. As a thank you for reading this book, Click Here to Get Your Copy of the '8 Week Blueprint on Building a Smart Home' - A summarized action plan, which you can follow over the coming weeks, months and indeed years.

Oh and if you are half thinking about making money out of installing smart home products then

>> Tap Here and Grab The Free Smart Home Install Toolkit

And finally as a reminder if you'd like to check out Gerard's course (and receive a 50% discount), here is the Link again.

Click Here to get over 50% discount off the regular price today before the **limited number of coupons run out!**

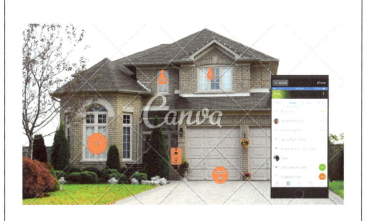

Essential Guide to Smart Home Automation Safety & Security

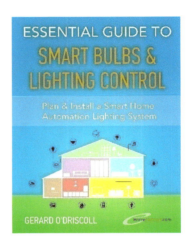

Essential Guide to Smart Bulbs & Lighting Control

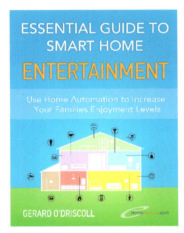

Essential Guide to Smart Home Entertainment

Essential Guide to Smart Homes For Aging Adults

Essential Guide to Nest Smart Home Automation System

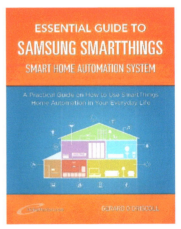

Essential Guide to Samsung SmartThings Smart Home Automation System

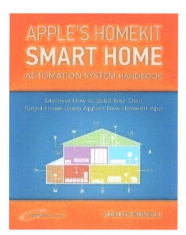

Essential Guide to Apple's HomeKit Smart
Home Automation System

Smart Home Automation Essential
Guides Box Set

A FAVOR!

If you loved the book and have a moment to spare, I would really appreciate a short review where you bought the book. The feedback will not only help sales but also provides me with encouragement to write books that identify how smart homes can enhance people's lives on a daily basis. If you do write a review, please send me an email at gerard@homementors.com and I'll give you the next book in the series for FREE!

Your help in spreading the word is gratefully appreciated.

Thanks.

www.ingramcontent.com/pod-product-compliance
Lightning Source LLC
Chambersburg PA
CBHW041433050326
40690CB00002B/523